GREAT SHORT POEMS

DOVER THRIFT EDITIONS

Edited by
Paul Negri

DOVER PUBLICATIONS, INC.
MINEOLA, NEW YORK

DOVER THRIFT EDITIONS

GENERAL EDITOR: PAUL NEGRI

❧

For Katherine and Marc

Copyright

Bibliographical Note

Great Short Poems is a new work, first published by Dover Publications, Inc., in 2000.

Library of Congress Cataloging-in-Publication Data

Great short poems / edited by Paul Negri.
    p. cm. — (Dover thrift editions)
  ISBN-13: 978-0-486-41105-7 (pbk.)
  ISBN-10: 0-486-41105-2 (pbk.)
  1. English poetry. 2. American poetry. I. Negri, Paul. II. Series.

PR1175 .G715 2000
821.008—dc21

                                    99-047784

Manufactured in the United States by RR Donnelley
41105214   2016
www.doverpublications.com

Note

Ben Jonson once said, "Even one verse alone sometimes makes a perfect poem." The truth of Jonson's assertion is amply evidenced in this collection of short poems. Here are works spanning 500 years of English and American literature, from Shakespeare to Robert Frost, richly diverse in sensibility, style and theme, but all with one salient feature in common—brevity.

Poetry is the art of compression, of saying in a few well-chosen words, enhanced with rhythm and musicality of language, what might take many more words to express—far less memorably—in prose. A good short poem pushes this art of compression to its limit. The 14 lines of Shakespeare's great sonnet "Let Me Not to the Marriage of True Minds" defines the nature of love with more truth and completeness than many weighty tomes on the subject. In "The Sick Rose," William Blake creates in 8 short lines a complex, multilayered lyric that could not have been more resonant with meaning if it had been hundreds of lines longer. Humorous and light verse, too, are often most effective in such small doses as Gelett Burgess's "The Purple Cow" and Leigh Hunt's "Jenny Kiss'd Me."

Most of the poems in this anthology are 16 lines or less (although a few have as many as 24 lines); many are no more than 8 or so lines. None take more than a minute or two to read. But within their brief scope, these verses encompass a world of sense and sentiment, present a distillation of often profound thought, and offer as large a measure of beauty and pleasure as works many times their length. To paraphrase the old adage, good (and even great) poems come in small packages.

Acknowledgments

T.S. Eliot: "Morning at the Window" and "The *Boston Evening Transcript*" from *Collected Poems 1909–1962* by T.S. Eliot. Copyright © 1936 by Harcourt Brace Jovanovich, Inc. Reprinted by permission of Faber and Faber Ltd.

Robert Frost: "Stopping by Woods on a Snowy Evening," "Fire and Ice," "The Road Not Taken," and "Acquainted with the Night" from *The Poetry of Robert Frost*, edited by Edward Connery Lathem. Copyright ©1951, 1956 by Robert Frost. Copyright 1923, 1928, ©1969 by Henry Holt and Company, LLC. Reprinted by permission of Henry Holt and Company and Jonathan Cape Ltd.

Langston Hughes: "The Negro Speaks of Rivers" from *Collected Poems* by Langston Hughes. Copyright ©1994 by the estate of Langston Hughes. Reprinted by permission of Alfred A. Knopf, a Division of Random House, Inc. and Harold Ober Associates, Inc.

Archibald MacLeish: "The End of the World" from *Collected Poems 1917–1982* by Archibald MacLeish. Copyright ©1985 by The Estate of Archibald MacLeish. Reprinted by permission of Houghton Mifflin Company. All rights reserved.

John Masefeild: "Sea Fever" from *The Poems and Plays of John Masefield* by John Masefield. Reprinted by permission of The Society of Authors as the literary representative of the Estate of John Masefield.

Edna St. Vincent Millay: "First Fig" and "Euclid Alone Has Looked on Beauty Bare" by Edna St. Vincent Millay. From *Collected Poems*, HarperCollins. Copyright ©1922, 1923, 1950, 1951 by Edna St. Vincent Millay and Norma Millay Ellis. All rights reserved. Reprinted by permission of Elizabeth Barnett, literary executor.

Wilfred Owen: "Anthem for Doomed Youth" from *The Collected Poems of Wilfred Owen*. Copyright ©1963 by Chatto & Windus, Ltd. Reprinted by permission of New Directions Publishing Corp.

Ezra Pound: "In a Station of a Metro" and "L'Art" from *Collected Shorter Poems* by Ezra Pound. Reprinted by permission of New Directions Publishing Corporation and Faber and Faber Ltd.

Wallace Stevens: "The Emperor of Ice Cream" and "Disillusionment of Ten O'Clock" from *Collected Poems* by Wallace Stevens. Copyright 1923, renewed 1951 by Wallace Stevens. Reprinted by permission of Alfred A. Knopf, Inc., and Faber and Faber Ltd.

Dylan Thomas: "Do Not Go Gentle Into That Good Night" from *The Poems of Dylan Thomas*. Copyright ©1952 by Dylan Thomas. Reprinted by permission of New Directions Publishing Corp. and David Higham Associates.

William Carlos Williams: "The Red Wheelbarrow" by William Carlos Williams. From *Collected Poems, 1909–1939, Vol.1*. Copyright ©1938 by New Directions Publishing Corp. Reprinted by permission of New Directions Publishing Corp. and Carcanet Press Ltd.

William Butler Yeats: "Leda and the Swan," "The Lake Isle of Innisfree," "Down by the Salley Gardens," and "When You are Old," by William Butler Yeats. From *The Collected Poems of W.B. Yeats*, Revised Second Edition edited by Richard J. Finneran. Copyright ©1928 by Macmillan Publishing Company, renewed 1956 by Georgie Yeats. Reprinted with the permission of A.P.Watt Ltd on behalf of Michael B. Yeats.

Contents

Contents

Sir Walter Ralegh (1554–1618)

Even Such Is Time

Even such is time that takes in trust
Our youth, our joys, our all we have,
And pays us but with age and dust,
Who in the dark and silent grave,
When we have wandered all our ways,
Shuts up the story of our days.
But from this earth, this grave, this dust,
My God shall raise me up, I trust.

William Shakespeare (1564–1616)

Shall I Compare Thee to a Summer's Day?

Shall I compare thee to a summer's day?
Thou art more lovely and more temperate:
Rough winds do shake the darling buds of May,
And summer's lease hath all too short a date;
Sometime too hot the eye of heaven shines,
And often is his gold complexion dimm'd;
And every fair from fair sometime declines,
By chance or nature's changing course untrimm'd:
But thy eternal summer shall not fade
Nor lose possession of that fair thou owest;
Nor shall Death brag thou wand'rest in his shade,
When in eternal lines to time thou growest'
　　So long as men can breathe or eyes can see,
　　So long lives this, and this gives life to thee.

When, in Disgrace with Fortune and Men's Eyes

When, in disgrace with fortune and men's eyes,
  I all alone beweep my outcast state,
And trouble deaf heaven with my bootless cries,
And look upon myself, and curse my fate,
Wishing me like to one more rich in hope,
Featured like him, like him with friends possessed,
Desiring this man's art, and that man's scope,
With what I most enjoy contented least;
Yet in these thoughts myself almost despising,
Haply I think on thee, and then my state,
Like to the lark at break of day arising
From sullen earth, sings hymns at heaven's gate;
  For thy sweet love remembered such wealth brings
  That then I scorn to change my state with kings.

Let Me Not to the Marriage of True Minds

Let me not to the marriage of true minds
Admit impediments. Love is not love
Which alters when it alteration finds,
Or bends with the remover to remove.
O, no! it is an ever-fixèd mark
That looks on tempests and is never shaken;
It is the star to every wand'ring bark,
Whose worth's unknown, although his height be taken.
Love's not Time's fool, though rosy lips and cheeks
Within his bending sickle's compass come;
Love alters not with his brief hours and weeks,
But bears it out even to the edge of doom.
  If this be error and upon me proved,
  I never writ, nor no man ever loved.

John Donne (1572–1631)

Death, Be Not Proud

Death, be not proud, though some have callèd thee
Mighty and dreadful, for thou art not so;
For those whom thou think'st thou dost overthrow
Die not, poor Death, nor yet canst thou kill me.
From rest and sleep, which but thy pictures be,
Much pleasure; then from thee much more must flow,

And soonest our best men with thee do go,
Rest of their bones, and soul's delivery.
Thou'rt slave to fate, chance, kings, and desperate men,
And dost with poison, war, and sickness dwell;
And poppy or charms can make us sleep as well
And better than thy stroke; why swell'st thou then?
One short sleep past, we wake eternally,
And death shall be no more: Death, thou shalt die.

Ben Jonson (1572–1637)

Drink to Me Only with Thine Eyes

Drink to me only with thine eyes,
   And I will pledge with mine;
Or leave a kiss but in the cup,
   And I'll not look for wine.
The thirst that from the soul doth rise
   Doth ask a drink divine;
But might I of Jove's nectar sup,
   I would not change for thine.
I sent thee late a rosy wreath,
   Not so much honoring thee
As giving it a hope that there
   It could not withered be.
But thou thereon didst only breathe,
   And sent'st it back to me;
Since when it grows, and smells, I swear,
   Not of itself, but thee.

John Webster (1580?–1634)

A Dirge

Call for the robin-redbreast and the wren,
Since o'er shady groves they hover,
And with leaves and flowers do cover
The friendless bodies of unburied men.
Call unto his funeral dole
The ant, the field-mouse, and the mole,
To rear him hillocks that shall keep him warm,
And (when gay tombs are robb'd) sustain no harm;
But keep the wolf far thence, that's foe to men,
For with his nails he'll dig them up again.

Robert Herrick (1591–1674)

To the Virgins, to Make Much of Time

Gather ye rose-buds while ye may,
  Old Time is still a-flying;
And this same flower that smiles today,
  Tomorrow will be dying.

The glorious lamp of heaven, the sun,
  The higher he's a-getting,
The sooner will his race be run,
  And nearer he's to setting.

That age is best which is the first,
  When youth and blood are warmer;
But being spent, the worse, and worst
  Times, still succeed the former.

Then be not coy, but use your time,
  And while ye may, go marry;
For having lost but once your prime,
  You may for ever tarry.

Upon Julia's Clothes

Whenas in silks my Julia goes,
Then, then, methinks, how sweetly flows
That liquefaction of her clothes.

Next, when I cast mine eyes and see
That brave vibration each way free,
O how that glittering taketh me!

Francis Quarles (1592–1644)

On the World

The world's an inn; and I her guest.
I eat; I drink; I take my rest.
My hostess, nature, does deny me
Nothing, wherewith she can supply me;
Where, having stayed a while, I pay
Her lavish bills, and go my way.

Thomas Carew (1595–1639)

The Unfading Beauty

He that loves a rosy cheek,
  Or a coral lip admires,
Or from star-like eyes doth seek
  Fuel to maintain his fires:
As old Time makes these decay,
So his flames must waste away.

But a smooth and steadfast mind,
  Gentle thoughts and calm desires,
Hearts with equal love combined,
  Kindle never-dying fires.
Where these are not, I despise
Lovely cheeks or lips or eyes.

John Milton (1608–1674)

On His Blindness

When I consider how my light is spent,
Ere half my days, in this dark world and wide,
And that one talent which is death to hide
Lodged with me useless, though my soul more bent
To serve therewith my Maker, and present
My true account, lest he returning chide,
"Doth God exact day labor, light denied?"
I fondly ask; by Patience, to prevent
That murmur, soon replies: "God doth not need
Either man's work or his own gifts; who best
Bear his mild yoke, they serve him best. His state
Is kingly: thousands at his bidding speed
And post o'er land and ocean without rest.
They also serve who only stand and wait."

Sir John Suckling (1609–1642)

Why So Pale and Wan, Fond Lover?

Why so pale and wan, fond lover?
    Prithee, why so pale?
Will, when looking well can't move her,
    Looking ill prevail?
    Prithee, why so pale?

Why so dull and mute, young sinner?
    Prithee, why so mute?
Will, when speaking well can't win her,
    Saying nothing do't?
    Prithee, why so mute?

Quit, quit, for shame; this will not move,
    This cannot take her.
If of herself she will not love,
    Nothing can make her:
    The devil take her!

Anne Bradstreet (1612–1672)

To My Dear and Loving Husband

If ever two were one, then surely we.
If ever man were loved by wife, then thee;
If ever wife was happy in a man,
Compare with me, ye women, if you can.
I prize thy love more than whole mines of gold,
Or all the riches that the East doth hold.
My love is such that rivers cannot quench,
Nor aught but love from thee give recompense.
Thy love is such I can no way repay;
The heavens reward thee manifold, I pray.
Then while we live, in love let's so persever,
That when we live no more we may live ever.

Richard Lovelace (1618–1658)

To Lucasta, Going to the Wars

Tell me not, Sweet, I am unkind
    That from the nunnery
Of thy chaste breast and quiet mind,
    To war and arms I fly.

True, a new mistress now I chase,
    The first foe in the field;
And with a stronger faith embrace
    A sword, a horse, a shield.

Yet this inconstancy is such
    As you too shall adore;
I could not love thee, Dear, so much,
Loved I not Honour more.

Sir George Etherege (1635–1691)

To a Lady Asking Him How Long He Would Love Her

It is not, Celia, in our power
    To say how long our love will last;
It may be we within this hour
    May lose those joys we now do taste;
The Blessèd, that immortal be,
From change in love are only free.

Then since we mortal lovers are,
    Ask not how long our love will last;
But while it does, let us take care
    Each minute be with pleasure past:
Were it not madness to deny
To live because we're sure to die?

Matthew Prior (1664–1721)

A Reasonable Affliction

On his death-bed poor Lubin lies:
　　His spouse is in despair;
With frequent cries, and mutual sighs,
　　They both express their care.

"A different cause," says Parson Sly,
　　"The same effect may give:
Poor Lubin fears that he may die;
　　His wife, that he may live."

Alexander Pope (1688–1744)

Ode on Solitude

Happy the man, whose wish and care
　　A few paternal acres bound,
Content to breathe his native air
　　　　　　In his own ground.

Whose herds with milk, whose fields with bread,
　　Whose flocks supply him with attire,
Whose trees in summer yield him shade,
　　　　　　In winter fire.

Blest, who can unconcern'dly find
　　Hours, days, and years slide soft away,
In health of body, peace of mind,
　　　　　　Quiet by day.

Sound sleep by night; study and ease,
　　Together mixt; sweet recreation:
And innocence, which most does please
　　　　　　With meditation.

Thus let me live, unseen, unknown,
　　Thus unlamented let me die,
Steal from the world, and not a stone
　　　　　　Tell where I lie.

John Gay (1688–1732)

Song

O ruddier than the cherry!
　O sweeter than the berry!
　O nymph more bright
　Than moonshine night,
Like kidlings blithe and merry!
Ripe as the melting cluster!
No lily has such lustre;
　Yet hard to tame
　As raging flame,
And fierce as storms that bluster!

Oliver Goldsmith (c. 1730–1774)

When Lovely Woman Stoops to Folly

When lovely woman stoops to folly,
　And finds too late that men betray,
What charm can soothe her melancholy,
　What art can wash her guilt away?

The only art her guilt to cover,
　To hide her shame from every eye,
To give repentance to her lover,
　And wring his bosom—is to die.

George Crabbe (1754–1832)

A Marriage Ring

The ring, so worn as you behold,
So thin, so pale, is yet of gold:
The passion such it was to prove—
Worn with life's care, love yet was love.

William Blake (1757–1827)

The Tiger

Tiger, Tiger, burning bright
In the forests of the night;
What immortal hand or eye,
Could frame thy fearful symmetry?

In what distant deeps or skies
Burnt the fire of thine eyes!
On what wings dare he aspire?
What the hand, dare seize the fire?

And what shoulder, & what art,
Could twist the sinews of thy heart?
And when thy heart began to beat,
What dread hand? & what dread feet?

What the hammer? what the chain?
In what furnace was thy brain?
What the anvil? what dread grasp
Dare its deadly terrors clasp?

When the stars threw down their spears
And water'd heaven with their tears:
Did he smile his work to see?
Did he who made the Lamb make thee?

Tiger, Tiger, burning bright,
In the forests of the night:
What immortal hand or eye,
Dare frame thy fearful symmetry?

Mock On, Mock On, Voltaire, Rousseau

Mock on, mock on, Voltaire, Rousseau;
Mock on, mock on, 'Tis all in vain.
You throw the sand against the wind,
And the wind blows it back again.

And every sand becomes a Gem
Reflected in the beams divine;
Blown back, they blind the mocking Eye,
But still in Israel's paths they shine.

The Atoms of Democritus
And Newton's Particles of light
Are sands upon the Red sea shore,
Where Israel's tents do shine so bright.

The Sick Rose

O Rose, thou art sick!
The invisible worm
That flies in the night,
In the howling storm,
Has found out thy bed
Of crimson joy:
And his dark secret love
Does thy life destroy.

Robert Burns (1759–1796)

A Red, Red Rose

O my Luve's like a red, red rose,
   That's newly sprung in June:
O my Luve's like the melodie
   That's sweetly played in tune!

As fair art thou, my bonnie lass,
   So deep in luve am I;
And I will luve thee still, my dear,
   Till a' the seas gang dry.

Till a' the seas gang dry, my dear,
   And the rocks melt wi' the sun;
I will luve thee still, my dear,
   While the sands o' life shall run.

And fare thee weel, my only Luve,
   And fare thee weel a while!
And I will come again, my Luve,
   Though it were ten thousand mile.

William Wordsworth (1770–1850)

I Wandered Lonely as a Cloud

I wandered lonely as a cloud
That floats on high o'er vales and hills,
When all at once I saw a crowd,
A host, of golden daffodils;
Beside the lake, beneath the trees,
Fluttering and dancing in the breeze.

Continuous as the stars that shine
And twinkle on the milky way,
They stretched in never-ending line
Along the margin of a bay:
Ten thousand saw I at a glance,
Tossing their heads in sprightly dance.

The waves beside them danced; but they
Out-did the sparkling waves in glee:
A poet could not but be gay,
In such a jocund company:
I gazed—and gazed—but little thought
What wealth the show to me had brought:

For oft, when on my couch I lie
In vacant or in pensive mood,
They flash upon that inward eye
Which is the bliss of solitude;
And then my heart with pleasure fills,
And dances with the daffodils.

My Heart Leaps Up

My heart leaps up when I behold
    A rainbow in the sky:
So was it when my life began;
So is it now I am a man;
So be it when I shall grow old,
    Or let me die!
The Child is father of the Man;
And I could wish my days to be
Bound each to each by natural piety.

She Dwelt Among the Untrodden Ways

She dwelt among the untrodden ways
   Beside the springs of Dove,
A Maid whom there were none to praise
   And very few to love:

A violet by a mossy stone
   Half hidden from the eye!
—Fair as a star, when only one
   Is shining in the sky.

She lived unknown, and few could know
   When Lucy ceased to be;
But she is in her grave, and, oh,
   The difference to me!

Walter Savage Landor (1775–1864)

Rose Aylmer

Ah, what avails the sceptred race!
   Ah, what the form divine!
What every virtue, every grace!
   Rose Aylmer, all were thine.

Rose Aylmer, whom these wakeful eyes
   May weep, but never see,
A night of memories and sighs
   I consecrate to thee.

Twenty Years Hence

Twenty years hence my eyes may grow,
If not quite dim, yet rather so;
Yet yours from others they shall know,
          Twenty years hence.

Twenty years hence, though it may hap
That I be call'd to take a nap
In a cool cell where thunder-clap
          Was never heard,

There breathe but o'er my arch of grass
A not too sadly sigh'd 'Alas!'
And I shall catch, ere you can pass,
                    That wingèd word.

Thomas Moore (1779–1852)

Believe Me, If All Those Endearing Young Charms

Believe me, if all those endearing young charms,
Which I gaze on so fondly to-day,
Were to change by to-morrow, and fleet in my arms,
Live fairy-gifts fading away,
Thou wouldst still be adored, as this moment thou art,
Let thy loveliness fade as it will,
And around the dear ruin each wish of my heart
Would entwine itself verdantly still.
It is not while beauty and youth are thine own,
And thy cheeks unprofaned by a tear,
That the fervor and faith of a soul may be known,
To which time will but make thee more dear!
No, the heart that has truly loved never forgets,
But as truly loves on to the close, ·
As the sunflower turns on her god when he sets
The same look which she turned when he rose!

Leigh Hunt (1784–1859)

Abou Ben Adhem

Abou Ben Adhem (may his tribe increase!)
Awoke one night from a deep dream of peace,
And saw, within the moonlight in his room,
Making it rich, and like a lily in bloom,
An angel writing in a book of gold:—
Exceeding peace had made Ben Adhem bold,
And to the presence in the room he said,
   'What writest thou?'—The vision rais'd its head,
And with a look made of all sweet accord,
Answer'd, 'The names of those who love the Lord.'
   'And is mine one?' asked Abou. 'Nay, not so,'
Replied the angel. Abou spoke more low,

But cheerly still; and said, 'I pray thee, then,
Write me as one that loves his fellow men.'
The angel wrote, and vanish'd. The next night
It came again with a great wakening light,
And show'd the names whom love of God had blest,
And lo! Ben Adhem's name led all the rest.

Jenny Kiss'd Me

Jenny kiss'd me when we met,
    Jumping from the chair she sat in;
Time, you thief, who love to get
    Sweets into your list, put that in!
Say I'm weary, say I'm sad,
    Say that health and wealth have miss'd me,
Say I'm growing old, but add,
    Jenny kiss'd me.

Thomas Love Peacock (1785–1866)

Beneath the Cypress Shade

I dug, beneath the cypress shade,
    What well might seem an elfin's grave;
And every pledge in earth I laid,
    That erst thy false affection gave.

I pressed them down the sod beneath;
    I placed one mossy stone above;
And twined the rose's fading wreath
    Around the sepulchre of love.

Frail as thy love, the flowers were dead,
    Ere yet the evening sun was set:
But years shall see the cypress spread,
    Immutable as my regret.

George Gordon, Lord Byron (1788–1824)

So We'll Go No More a-Roving

So, we'll go no more a-roving
    So late into the night,
Though the heart be still as loving,
    And the moon be still as bright.

For the sword outwears its sheath,
　　And the soul outwears the breast,
And the heart must pause to breathe,
　　And love itself have rest.

Though the night was made for loving,
　　And the day returns too soon,
Yet we'll go no more a-roving
　　By the light of the moon.

She Walks in Beauty

I

She walks in Beauty, like the night
　　Of cloudless climes and starry skies;
And all that's best of dark and bright
　　Meet in her aspect and her eyes:
Thus mellowed to that tender light
　　Which Heaven to gaudy day denies.

II

One shade the more, one ray the less,
　　Had half impaired the nameless grace
Which waves in every raven tress,
　　Or softly lightens o'er her face;
Where thoughts serenely sweet express,
　　How pure, how dear their dwelling-place.

III

And on that cheek, and o'er that brow,
　　So soft, so calm, yet eloquent,
The smiles that win, the tints that glow,
　　But tell of days in goodness spent,
A mind at peace with all below,
　　A heart whose love is innocent!

Percy Bysshe Shelley (1792–1822)

Ozymandias

I met a traveler from an antique land
Who said: Two vast and trunkless legs of stone
Stand in the desert. Near them, on the sand,
Half sunk, a shattered visage lies, whose frown,
And wrinkled lip, and sneer of cold command,

Tell that its sculptor well those passions read
Which yet survive, stamped on these lifeless things,
The hand that mocked them and the heart that fed;
And on the pedestal these words appear:
"My name is Ozymandias, king of kings:
Look on my works, ye Mighty, and despair!"
Nothing beside remains. Round the decay
Of that colossal wreck, boundless and bare
The lone and level sands stretch far away.

John Keats (1795–1821)

When I Have Fears

When I have fears that I may cease to be
    Before my pen has gleaned my teeming brain,
Before high-piled books, in charactery,
    Hold like rich garners the full ripened·grain;
When I behold, upon the night's starred face,
    Huge cloudy symbols of a high romance,
And think that I may never live to trace
    Their shadows, with the magic hand of chance;
And when I feel, fair creature of an hour,
    That I shall never look upon thee more,
Never have relish in the faery power
    Of unreflecting love;—then on the shore
Of the wide world I stand alone, and think
Till love and fame to nothingness do sink.

Hartley Coleridge (1796–1849)

Song

She is not fair to outward view
    As many maidens be,
Her loveliness I never knew
    Until she smiled on me;
O, then I saw her eye was bright,
A well of love, a spring of light!

But now her looks are coy and cold,
To mine they ne'er reply,
And yet I cease not to behold

The love-light in her eye:
Her very frowns are fairer far
Than smiles of other maidens are.

Early Death

She pass'd away like morning dew
    Before the sun was high;
So brief her time, she scarcely knew
    The meaning of a sigh.

As round the rose its soft perfume,
    Sweet love around her floated;
Admired she grew—while mortal doom
    Crept on, unfear'd, unnoted.

Love was her guardian Angel here,
    But Love to Death resign'd her;
Tho' Love was kind, why should we fear
    But holy Death is kinder?

Thomas Hood (1799–1845)

The Death-Bed

We watch'd her breathing thro' the night,
    Her breathing soft and low,
As in her breast the wave of life
    Kept heaving to and fro.

So silently we seem'd to speak,
    So slowly moved about,
As we had lent her half our powers
    To eke her living out.

Our very hopes belied our fears,
    Our fears our hopes belied—
We thought her dying when she slept,
    And sleeping when she died.

For when the morn came dim and sad,
    And chill with early showers,
Her quiet eyelids closed—she had
    Another morn than ours.

Ralph Waldo Emerson (1803–1882)

Days

Daughters of Time, the hypocritic Days,
Muffled and dumb like barefoot dervishes,
And marching single in an endless file,
Bring diadems and faggots in their hands.
To each they offer gifts after his will,
Bread, kingdoms, stars, and sky that holds them all.
I, in my pleached garden, watched the pomp,
Forgot my morning wishes, hastily
Took a few herbs and apples, and the Day
Turned and departed silent. I, too late,
Under her solemn fillet saw the scorn.

Character

The sun set, but set not his hope:
Stars rose; his faith was earlier up:
Fixed on the enormous galaxy,
Deeper and older seemed his eye;
And matched his sufferance sublime
The taciturnity of time.
He spoke, and words more soft than rain
Brought the Age of Gold again:
His action won such reverence sweet
As hid all measure of the feat.

Elizabeth Barrett Browning (1806–1861)

How Do I Love Thee? Let Me Count the Ways

How do I love thee? Let me count the ways.
I love thee to the depth and breadth and height
My soul can reach, when feeling out of sight
For the ends of Being and ideal Grace.
I love thee to the level of every day's
Most quiet need; by sun and candle-light.
I love thee freely, as men strive for Right;
I love thee purely, as they turn from Praise.
I love thee with the passion put to use

In my old griefs, and with my childhood's faith.
I love thee with a love I seemed to lose
With my lost saints,—I love thee with the breath.
Smiles, tears, of all my life!—and, if God choose,
I shall but love thee better after death.

Henry Wadsworth Longfellow (1807–1882)

The Arrow and the Song

I shot an arrow into the air,
It fell to earth, I knew not where;
For, so swiftly it flew, the sight
Could not follow it in its flight.

I breathed a song into the air,
It fell to earth, I knew not where;
For who has sight so keen and strong,
That it can follow the flight of song?

Long, long afterward, in an oak
I found the arrow, still unbroke;
And the song, from beginning to end,
I found again in the heart of a friend.

There Was a Little Girl

There was a little girl, she had a little curl
    Right in the middle of her forehead;
And when she was good, she was very, very good,
    And when she was bad, she was horrid.

Edgar Allan Poe (1809–1849)

To One in Paradise

Thou wast all that to me, love,
    For which my soul did pine—
A green isle in the sea, love,
    A fountain and a shrine,
All wreathed with fairy fruits and flowers,
    And all the flowers were mine.

Now all my days are trances,
    And all my nightly dreams

> Are where thy grey eye glances,
>> And where thy footstep gleams—
> In what ethereal dances,
>> By what eternal streams!

Alfred, Lord Tennyson (1809–1892)

The Splendor Falls

The splendor falls on castle walls
    And snowy summits old in story;
The long light shakes across the lakes,
    And the wild cataract leaps in glory.
Blow, bugle, blow, set the wild echoes flying,
Blow, bugle; answer, echoes, dying, dying, dying.

O, hark, O, hear! how thin and clear,
    And thinner, clearer, farther going!
O, sweet and far from cliff and scar
    The horns of Elfland faintly blowing!
Blow, let us hear the purple glens replying,
Blow, bugle; answer, echoes, dying, dying, dying.

Crossing the Bar

Sunset and evening star,
    And one clear call for me!
And may there be no moaning of the bar,
    When I put out to sea,

But such a tide as moving seems asleep,
    Too full for sound and foam,
When that which drew from out the boundless deep
    Turns again home.

Twilight and evening bell,
    And after that the dark!
And may there be no sadness of farewell,
    When I embark;

For though from out our bourne of Time and Place
    The flood may bear me far,
I hope to see my Pilot face to face
    When I have crossed the bar.

The Eagle

He clasps the crag with crooked hands;
Close to the sun in lonely lands,
Ringed with the azure world, he stands.

The wrinkled sea beneath him crawls;
He watches from his mountain walls,
And like a thunderbolt he falls.

Flower in the Crannied Wall

Flower in the crannied wall,
I pluck you out of the crannies,
I hold you here, root and all, in my hand,
Little flower—but *if* I could understand
What you are, root and all, and all in all,
I should know what God and man is.

Edward FitzGerald (1809–1883)

The Three Arrows

PORCIA'S SONG
Of all the shafts to Cupid's bow,
    The first is tipp'd with fire;
All bare their bosoms to the blow
    And call the wound Desire.

Love's second is a poison'd dart,
    And Jealousy is named:
Which carries poison to the heart
    Desire had first inflamed.

The last of Cupid's arrows all
    With heavy lead is set:
That vainly weeping lovers call
    Repentance, or Regret.

Robert Browning (1812–1889)

Meeting at Night

I

The gray sea and the long black land;
And the yellow half-moon large and low;
And the startled little waves that leap
In fiery ringlets from their sleep,
As I gain the cove with pushing prow,
And quench its speed i' the slushy sand.

II

Then a mile of warm sea-scented beach;
Three fields to cross till a farm appears;
A tap at the pane, the quick sharp scratch
And blue spurt of a lighted match,
And a voice less loud, thro' its joys and fears,
Than the two hearts beating each to each!

Parting at Morning

Round the cape of a sudden came the sea,
And the sun looked over the mountain's rim:
And straight was a path of gold for him,
And the need of a world of men for me.

Pippa's Song

The year's at the spring,
And day's at the morn;
Morning's at seven;
The hill-side's dew-pearl'd;
The lark's on the wing;
The snail's on the thorn;
God's in his heaven—
All's right with the world!

Henry David Thoreau (1817–1862)

I Was Born Upon Thy Bank, River

I was born upon thy bank, river,
  My blood flows in thy stream,
And thou meanderest forever
  At the bottom of my dream.

My Life Has Been the Poem

My life has been the poem I would have writ,
But I could not both live and utter it.

Emily Brontë (1818–1848)

The Old Stoic

Riches I hold in light esteem;
  And Love I laugh to scorn;
And lust of fame was but a dream
  That vanished with the morn:

And if I pray, the only prayer
  That moves my lips for me
Is, "Leave the heart that now I bear,
  And give me liberty!"

Yes, as my swift days near their goal,
  'Tis all that I implore;
In life and death, a chainless soul,
  With courage to endure.

Arthur Hugh Clough (1819–1861)

Say Not the Struggle Nought Availeth

Say not the struggle nought availeth,
  The labor and the wounds are vain,
The enemy faints not, nor faileth,
  And as things have been they remain.

If hopes were dupes, fears may be liars;
  It may be, in yon smoke concealed,
Your comrades chase e'en now the fliers,
  And, but for you, possess the field.

For while the tired waves, vainly breaking,
    Seem here no painful inch to gain,
Far back through creeks and inlets making,
    Coming silent, flooding in, the main.

And not by eastern windows only,
    When daylight comes, comes in the light,
In front the sun climbs slow, how slowly,
    But westward, look, the land is bright.

Walt Whitman (1819–1892)

A Noiseless Patient Spider

A noiseless patient spider,
I mark'd where on a little promontory it stood isolated,
Mark'd how to explore the vacant vast surrounding,
It launch'd forth filament, filament, filament, out of itself,
Ever unreeling them, ever tirelessly speeding them.

And you O my soul where you stand,
Surrounded, detached, in measureless oceans of space,
Ceaselessly musing, venturing, throwing, seeking the spheres
    to connect them,
Till the bridge you will need be form'd, till the ductile anchor hold,
Till the gossamer thread you fling catch somewhere, O, my soul.

I Hear America Singing

I hear America singing, the varied carols I hear,
Those of mechanics, each one singing his as it should be blithe
    and strong,
The carpenter singing his as he measures his plank or beam,
The mason singing his as he makes ready for work, or leaves off work,
The boatman singing what belongs to him in his boat, the deckhand
    singing on the steamboat deck,
The shoemaker singing as he sits on his bench, the hatter singing
    as he stands,
The wood-cutter's song, the plowboy's on his way in the morning,
    or at noon intermission or at sundown,
The delicious singing of the mother, or of the young wife at work,
    or of the girl sewing or washing,
Each singing what belongs to him or her and to none else,
The day what belongs to the day—at night the party of young fellows,
    robust, friendly,
Singing with open mouths their strong melodious songs.

Coventry Patmore (1823–1896)

The Kiss

'I saw you take his kiss!' ''Tis true.'
  'O modesty!' ''Twas strictly kept:
He thought me asleep—at least, I knew
  He thought I thought he thought I slept.'

Magna Est Veritas

Here, in this little Bay,
Full of tumultuous life and great repose,
Where, twice a day,
The purposeless, glad ocean comes and goes,
Under high cliffs, and far from the huge town,
I sit me down.
For want of me the world's course will not fail:
When all its work is done, the lie shall rot;
The truth is great, and shall prevail,
When none cares whether it prevail or not.

George Meredith (1818–1909)

Lucifer in Starlight

On a starred night Prince Lucifer uprose.
  Tired of his dark dominion, swung the fiend
  Above the rolling ball in cloud part screened,
Where sinners hugged their specter of repose.
Poor prey to his hot fit of pride were those.
  And now upon his western wing he leaned,
  Now his huge bulk o'er Afric's sands careened,
Now the black planet shadowed Arctic snows.
Soaring through wider zones that pricked his scars
  With memory of the old revolt from Awe,
He reached a middle height, and at the stars,
Which are the brain of heaven, he looked, and sank.
Around the ancient track marched, rank on rank,
  The army of unalterable law.

Emily Dickinson (1830–1886)

I Heard a Fly Buzz When I Died

I heard a fly buzz when I died;
   The stillness round my form
Was like the stillness in the air
   Between the heaves of storm.

The eyes beside had wrung them dry,
   And breaths were gathering sure
For that last onset, when the king
   Be witnessed in his power.

I willed my keepsakes, signed away
   What portion of me I
Could make assignable,—and then
   There interposed a fly,

With blue, uncertain, stumbling buzz,
   Between the light and me;
And then the windows failed, and then
   I could not see to see.

The Soul Selects Her Own Society

The soul selects her own society,
Then shuts the door;
On her divine majority
Obtrude no more.

Unmoved, she notes the chariot's pausing
At her low gate;
Unmoved, an emperor is kneeling
Upon her mat.

I've known her from an ample nation
Choose one;
Then close the valves of her attention
Like stone.

My Life Closed Twice Before Its Close

My life closed twice before its close;
   It yet remains to see
If Immortality unveil
   A third event to me,

So huge, so hopeless to conceive,
   As these that twice befell.
Parting is all we know of heaven,
   And all we need of hell.

I Never Saw a Moor

I never saw a moor,
I never saw the sea;
Yet know I how the heather looks,
And what a wave must be.

I never spoke with God,
Nor visited in heaven;
Yet certain am I of the spot
As if the chart were given.

Christina Rossetti (1830–1894)

Remember

Remember me when I am gone away,
   Gone far away into the silent land;
   When you can no more hold me by the hand,
Nor I half turn to go yet turning stay.
Remember me when no more day by day
   You tell me of our future that you planned:
   Only remember me; you understand
It will be late to counsel then or pray.
Yet if you should forget me for a while
   And afterwards remember, do not grieve:
   For if the darkness and corruption leave
A vestige of the thoughts that once I had,
Better by far you should forget and smile
   Than that you should remember and be sad.

Up-Hill

Does the road wind up-hill all the way?
   Yes, to the very end.
Will the day's journey take the whole long day?
   From morn to night, my friend.

But is there for the night a resting-place?
   A roof for when the slow dark hours begin.

May not the darkness hide it from my face?
   You cannot miss that inn.

Shall I meet other wayfarers at night?
   Those who have gone before.
Then must I knock, or call when just in sight?
   They will not keep you standing at that door.

Shall I find comfort, travel-sore and weak?
   Of labour you shall find the sum.
Will there be beds for me and all who seek?
   Yea, beds for all who come.

Lewis Carroll (1832–1898)

How Doth the Little Crocodile

How doth the little crocodile
   Improve his shining tail,
And pour the waters of the Nile
   On every golden scale!

How cheerfully he seems to grin,
   How neatly spreads his claws,
And welcomes little fishes in
   With gently smiling jaws!

Thomas Bailey Aldrich (1836–1906)

Memory

My mind lets go a thousand things,
Like dates of wars and deaths of kings,
And yet recalls the very hour—
'T was noon by yonder village tower,
And on the last blue noon in May—
The wind came briskly up this way,
Crisping the brook beside the road;
Then, pausing here, set down its load
Of pine-scents, and shook listlessly
Two petals from that wild-rose tree.

Thomas Hardy (1840–1928)

Hap

If but some vengeful god would call to me
From up the sky, and laugh: 'Thou suffering thing,
Know that thy sorrow is my ecstasy,
That thy love's loss is my hate's profiting!'

Then would I bear it, clench myself, and die,
Steeled by the sense of ire unmerited;
Half-eased in that a Powerfuller than I
Had willed and meted me the tears I shed.

But not so. How arrives it joy lies slain,
And why unblooms the best hope ever sown?
—Crass Casualty obstructs the sun and rain,
And dicing Time for gladness casts a moan. . . .
These purblind Doomsters had as readily strown
Blisses about my pilgrimage as pain.

In Time of 'The Breaking of Nations'

I
Only a man harrowing clods
    In a slow silent walk
With an old horse that stumbles and nods
    Half asleep as they stalk.

II
Only thin smoke without flame
    From the heaps of couch-grass;
Yet this will go onward the same
    Though Dynasties pass.

III
Yonder a maid and her wight
    Come whispering by:
War's annals will cloud into night
    Ere their story die.

I Look into My Glass

I look into my glass,
And view my wasting skin,
And say, 'Would God it came to pass
My heart had shrunk as thin!'

For then, I, undistrest
By hearts grown cold to me,
Could lonely wait my endless rest
With equanimity.

But Time, to make me grieve,
Part steals, lets part abide;
And shakes this fragile frame at eve
With throbbings of noontide.

Gerard Manley Hopkins (1844–1889)

Pied Beauty

Glory be to God for dappled things—
　　For skies of couple-colour as a brinded cow;
　　　　For rose-moles all in stipple upon trout that swim;
Fresh-firecoal chestnut-falls; finches' wings;
　　Landscape plotted and pieced—fold, fallow, and plough;
　　　　And áll trádes, their gear and tackle and trim.
All things counter, original, spare, strange;
　　Whatever is fickle, freckled (who knows how?)
　　　　With swift, slow; sweet, sour; adazzle, dim;
He fathers-forth whose beauty is past change:
　　　　Praise him.

God's Grandeur

The world is charged with the grandeur of God.
　　It will flame out, like shining from shook foil;
　　It gathers to a greatness, like the ooze of oil
Crushed. Why do men then now not reck his rod?
Generations have trod, have trod, have trod;
　　And all is seared with trade; bleared, smeared with toil;
　　And wears man's smudge and shares man's smell: the soil
Is bare now, nor can foot feel, being shod.

And for all this, nature is never spent;
　　There lives the dearest freshness deep down things;
And though the last lights off the black West went
　　Oh, morning, at the brown brink eastward, springs—
Because the Holy Ghost over the bent
　　World broods with warm breast and with ah! bright wings.

No Worst, There Is None

No worst, there is none. Pitched past pitch of grief,
More pangs will, schooled at forepangs, wilder wring.
Comforter, where, where is your comforting?
Mary, mother of us, where is your relief?
My cries heave, herds-long; huddle in a main, a chief-
woe, world-sorrow; on an age-old anvil wince and sing—
Then lull, then leave off. Fury had shrieked "No ling-
ering! Let me be fell: force I must be brief."
O the mind, mind has mountains; cliffs of fall
Frightful, sheer, no-man-fathomed. Hold them cheap
May who ne'er hung there. Nor does long our small
Durance deal with that steep or deep. Here! creep,
Wretch, under a comfort serves in a whirlwind: all
Life death does end and each day dies with sleep.

John Banister Tabb (1845–1909)

Evolution

Out of the dusk a shadow,
    Then, a spark;
Out of the cloud a silence,
    Then, a lark;
Out of the heart a rapture,
    Then, a pain;
Out of the dead, cold ashes,
    Life again.

The Shadow

O Shadow, in thy fleeting form I see
The friend of fortune that once clung to me.
In flattering light, thy constancy is shown;
In darkness, thou wilt leave me all alone.

The Mid-Day Moon

Behold, whatever wind prevail,
Slow westering, a phantom sail—
The lonely soul of Yesterday—
Unpiloted, pursues her way.

Emma Lazarus (1849–1887)

The New Colossus

Not like the brazen giant of Greek fame,
With conquering limbs astride from land to land;
Here at our sea-washed, sunset gates shall stand
A mighty woman with a torch, whose flame
Is the imprisoned lightning, and her name
Mother of Exiles. From her beacon-hand
Glows world-wide welcome; her mild eyes command
The air-bridged harbor that twin cities frame.
"Keep, ancient lands, your storied pomp!" cries she
With silent lips. "Give me your tired, your poor,
Your huddled masses yearning to breathe free,
The wretched refuse of your teeming shore.
Send these, the homeless, tempest-tost to me,
I lift my lamp beside the golden door!"

William Ernest Henley (1849–1903)

Invictus

Out of the night that covers me,
    Black as the pit from pole to pole,
I thank whatever gods may be
    For my unconquerable soul.

In the fell clutch of circumstance
    I have not winced nor cried aloud.
Under the bludgeonings of chance
    My head is bloody, but unbowed.

Beyond this place of wrath and tears
    Looms but the Horror of the shade,
And yet the menace of the years
    Finds and shall find me unafraid.

It matters not how strait the gate,
    How charged with punishments the scroll,
I am the master of my fate:
    I am the captain of my soul.

Robert Louis Stevenson (1850–1894)

Requiem

Under the wide and starry sky,
Dig the grave and let me lie.
Glad did I live and gladly die,
    And I laid me down with a will.

This be the verse you grave for me:
Here he lies where he longed to be;
Home is the sailor, home from the sea,
    And the hunter home from the hill.

Francis William Bourdillon (1852–1921)

The Night Has a Thousand Eyes

The night has a thousand eyes,
    And the day but one;
Yet the light of the bright world dies
    With the dying sun.

The mind has a thousand eyes,
    And the heart but one;
Yet the light of a whole life dies
    When love is done.

Ella Wheeler Wilcox (1850–1919)

Solitude

Laugh, and the world laughs with you;
    Weep, and you weep alone.
For the sad old earth must borrow its mirth,
    But has trouble enough of its own.
Sing, and the hills will answer;
    Sigh, it is lost on the air.
The echoes bound to a joyful sound,
    But shrink from voicing care.

Rejoice, and men will seek you;
    Grieve, and they turn and go.
They want full measure of all your pleasure,
    But they do not need your woe.

Be glad, and your friends are many;
    Be sad, and you lose them all.
There are none to decline your nectared wine,
    But alone you must drink life's gall.

Feast, and your halls are crowded;
    Fast, and the world goes by.
Succeed and give, and it helps you live,
    But no man can help you die.
There is room in the halls of pleasure
    For a long and lordly train,
But one by one we must all file on
    Through the narrow aisles of pain.

The Winds of Fate

One ship drives east and another drives west
    With the selfsame winds that blow.
        'Tis the set of the sails
        And not the gales
Which tells us the way to go.

Like the winds of the sea are the ways of fate,
    As we voyage along through life:
        'Tis the set of a soul
        That decides its goal,
And not the calm or the strife.

Oscar Wilde (1854–1900)

E Tenebris

Come down, O Christ, and help me! reach thy hand,
    For I am drowning in a stormier sea
    Than Simon on thy lake of Galilee:
The wine of life is spilt upon the sand,
My heart is as some famine-murdered land
    Whence all good things have perished utterly,
    And well I know my soul in Hell must lie
If I this night before God's throne should stand.
"He sleeps perchance, or rideth to the chase,
    Like Baal, when his prophets howled that name
    From morn to noon on Carmel's smitten height."
Nay, peace, I shall behold, before the night,

The feet of brass, the robe more white than flame,
The wounded hands, the weary human face.

Symphony in Yellow

An omnibus across the bridge
    Crawls like a yellow butterfly,
    And, here and there, a passer-by
Shows like a little restless midge.

Big barges full of yellow hay
    Are moved against the shadowy wharf,
    And, like a yellow silken scarf,
The thick fog hangs along the quay.

The yellow leaves begin to fade
    And flutter from the Temple elms,
    And at my feet the pale green Thames
Lies like a rod of rippled jade.

John Davidson (1857–1909)

Song

The boat is chafing at our long delay,
    And we must leave too soon
The spicy sea-pinks and the inborne spray,
    The tawny sands, the moon.

Keep us, O Thetis, in our western flight!
    Watch from thy pearly throne
Our vessel, plunging deeper into night
    To reach a land unknown.

A. E. Housman (1859–1936)

When I Was One-and-Twenty

When I was one-and-twenty
    I heard a wise man say,
"Give crowns and pounds and guineas
    But not your heart away;
Give pearls away and rubies
    But keep your fancy free."

But I was one-and-twenty,
    No use to talk to me.

When I was one-and-twenty
    I heard him say again,
"The heart out of the bosom
    Was never given in vain;
'Tis paid with sighs a plenty
    And sold for endless rue."
And I am two-and-twenty,
    And oh, 'tis true, 'tis true.

Into My Heart an Air That Kills

Into my heart an air that kills
    From yon far country blows:
What are those blue remembered hills,
    What spires, what farms are those?

That is the land of lost content,
    I see it shining plain,
The happy highways where I went
    And cannot come again.

With Rue My Heart Is Laden

With rue my heart is laden
    For golden friends I had,
For many a rose-lipt maiden
    And many a lightfoot lad.

By brooks too broad for leaping
    The lightfoot boys are laid;
The rose-lipt girls are sleeping
    In fields where roses fade.

Loveliest of Trees

Loveliest of trees, the cherry now
Is hung with bloom along the bough,
And stands about the woodland ride
Wearing white for Eastertide.

Now, of my threescore years and ten,
Twenty will not come again,

And take from seventy springs a score,
It only leaves me fifty more.

And since to look at things in bloom
Fifty springs are little room,
About the woodlands I will go
To see the cherry hung with snow.

William Butler Yeats (1865–1939)

Leda and the Swan

A sudden blow: the great wings beating still
Above the staggering girl, her thighs caressed
By the dark webs, her nape caught in his bill,
He holds her helpless breast upon his breast.

How can those terrified vague fingers push
The feathered glory from her loosening thighs?
And how can body, laid in that white rush,
But feel the strange heart beating where it lies?

A shudder in the loins engenders there
The broken wall, the burning roof and tower
And Agamemnon dead.
       Being so caught up,
So mastered by the brute blood of the air,
Did she put on his knowledge with his power
Before the indifferent beak could let her drop?

The Lake Isle of Innisfree

I will arise and go now, and go to Innisfree,
And a small cabin build there, of clay and wattles made:
Nine bean-rows will I have there, a hive for the honey-bee,
And live alone in the bee-loud glade.

And I shall have some peace there, for peace comes dropping slow,
Dropping from the veils of the morning to where the cricket sings;
There midnight's all a glimmer, and noon a purple glow,
And evening full of the linnet's wings.

And I will arise and go now, for always night and day
I hear the lake water lapping with low sounds by the shore;
While I stand on the roadway, or on the pavements gray,
I hear it in the deep heart's core.

Down by the Salley Gardens

Down by the salley gardens my love and I did meet;
She pass'd the salley gardens with little snow-white feet.
She bid me take love easy, as the leaves grow on the tree;
But I, being young and foolish, with her would not agree.

In a field by the river my love and I did stand,
And on my leaning shoulder she laid her snow-white hand.
She bid me take life easy, as the grass grows on the weirs;
But I was young and foolish, and now am full of tears.

When You Are Old

When you are old and gray and full of sleep,
And nodding by the fire, take down this book,
And slowly read, and dream of the soft look
Your eyes had once, and of their shadows deep;

How many loved your moments of glad grace,
And loved your beauty with love false or true,
But one man loved the pilgrim soul in you,
And loved the sorrows of your changing face;

And bending down beside the glowing bars,
Murmur, a little sadly, how love fled
And paced upon the mountains overhead
And hid his face amid a crowd of stars.

Gelett Burgess (1866–1951)

The Purple Cow

I never saw a Purple Cow,
    I never hope to see one;
But I can tell you, anyhow,
    I'd rather see than be one.

Cinq Ans Après

Ah, yes! I wrote the "Purple Cow"—
    I'm sorry, now, I wrote it!
But I can tell you, anyhow,
    I'll kill you if you quote it!

Ernest Dowson (1867–1900)

Non Sum Qualis Eram Bonae sub Regno Cynarae

Last night, ah, yesternight, betwixt her lips and mine
There fell thy shadow, Cynara! thy breath was shed
Upon my soul between the kisses and the wine;
And I was desolate and sick of an old passion,
    Yea, I was desolate and bowed my head:
I have been faithful to thee, Cynara! in my fashion.

All night upon mine heart I felt her warm heart beat,
Night-long within mine arms in love and sleep she lay;
Surely the kisses of her bought red mouth were sweet;
But I was desolate and sick of an old passion,
    When I awoke and found the dawn was gray:
I have been faithful to thee, Cynara! in my fashion.

I have forgot much, Cynara! gone with the wind,
Flung roses, roses riotously with the throng,
Dancing, to put thy pale, lost lilies out of mind;
But I was desolate and sick of an old passion,
    Yea, all the time, because the dance was long:
I have been faithful to thee, Cynara! in my fashion.

Envoy

They are not long, the weeping and the laughter,
Love and desire and hate;
I think they have no portion in us after
    We pass the gate.

They are not long, the days of wine and roses:
Out of a misty dream
Our path emerges for a while, then closes
    Within a dream.

E. A. Robinson (1869–1935)

Richard Cory

Whenever Richard Cory went down town,
We people on the pavement looked at him:
He was a gentleman from sole to crown,
Clean favored, and imperially slim.

And he was always quietly arrayed,
And he was always human when he talked;

But still he fluttered pulses when he said,
"Good-morning," and he glittered when he walked.

And he was rich—yes, richer than a king—
And admirably schooled in every grace:
In fine, we thought that he was everything
To make us wish that we were in his place.

So on we worked, and waited for the light,
And went without the meat, and cursed the bread;
And Richard Cory, one calm summer night,
Went home and put a bullet through his head.

Eros Turannos

She fears him, and will always ask
  What fated her to choose him;
She meets in his engaging mask
  All reasons to refuse him;
But what she meets and what she fears
Are less than are the downward years,
Drawn slowly to the foamless weirs
  Of age, were she to lose him.

Between a blurred sagacity
  That once had power to sound him,
And Love, that will not let him be
  The Judas that she found him,
Her pride assuages her almost,
As if it were alone the cost.—
He sees that he will not be lost,
  And waits and looks around him.

Stephen Crane (1871–1900)

"I Saw a Man Pursuing the Horizon"

I saw a man pursuing the horizon;
Round and round they sped.
I was disturbed at this;
I accosted the man.
"It is futile," I said,
"You can never—"
"You lie," he cried,
And ran on.

"In the Desert"

In the desert
I saw a creature, naked, bestial,
Who, squatting upon the ground,
Held his heart in his hands,
And ate of it.
I said, "Is it good, friend?"
It is bitter—bitter," he answered;
"But I like it
"Because it is bitter,
"And because it is my heart."

"A Learned Man Came to Me Once"

A learned man came to me once.
He said, "I know the way,—come."
And I was overjoyed at this.
Together we hastened.
Soon, too soon, were we
Where my eyes were useless,
And I knew not the ways of my feet.
I clung to the hand of my friend;
But at last he cried, "I am lost."

Paul Laurence Dunbar (1872–1906)

Life

A crust of bread and a corner to sleep in,
A minute to smile and an hour to weep in,
A pint of joy to a peck of trouble,
And never a laugh but the moans come double;
    And that is life!

A crust and a corner that love makes precious,
With a smile to warm and the tears to refresh us;
And joy seems sweeter when cares come after,
And a moan is the finest of foils for laughter;
    And that is life!

We Wear the Mask

We wear the mask that grins and lies,
It hides our cheeks and shades our eyes,—
This debt we pay to human guile;
With torn and bleeding hearts we smile,
And mouth with myriad subtleties.

Why should the world be overwise,
In counting all our tears and sighs?
Nay, let them only see us, while
     We wear the mask.

We smile, but, O great Christ, our cries
To thee from tortured souls arise.
We sing, but oh the clay is vile
Beneath our feet, and long the mile;
But let the world dream otherwise,
     We wear the mask!

Silence

'T is better to sit here beside the sea,
    Here on the spray-kissed beach,
In silence, that between such friends as we
    Is full of deepest speech.

Amy Lowell (1874–1925)

Solitaire

When night drifts along the streets of the city,
And sifts down between the uneven roofs,
My mind begins to peek and peer.
It plays at ball in old, blue Chinese gardens,
And shakes wrought dice-cups in Pagan temples,
Amid the broken flutings of white pillars.
It dances with purple and yellow crocuses in its hair,
And its feet shine as they flutter over drenched grasses.
How light and laughing my mind is,
When all the good folk have put out their bed-room candles,
And the city is still!

Robert Frost (1874–1963)

Stopping by Woods on a Snowy Evening

Whose woods these are I think I know.
His house is in the village, though;
He will not see me stopping here
To watch his woods fill up with snow.

My little horse must think it queer
To stop without a farmhouse near
Between the woods and frozen lake
The darkest evening of the year.

He gives his harness bells a shake
To ask if there is some mistake.
The only other sound's the sweep
Of easy wind and downy flake.

The woods are lovely, dark, and deep,
But I have promises to keep,
And miles to go before I sleep,
And miles to go before I sleep.

Fire and Ice

Some say the world will end in fire,
Some say in ice.
From what I've tasted of desire
I hold with those who favor fire.
But if it had to perish twice,
I think I know enough of hate
To say that for destruction ice
Is also great
And would suffice.

The Road Not Taken

Two roads diverged in a yellow wood,
And sorry I could not travel both
And be one traveler, long I stood
And looked down one as far as I could
To where it bent in the undergrowth;

Then took the other, as just as fair,
And having perhaps the better claim,

Because it was grassy and wanted wear;
Though as for that the passing there
Had worn them really about the same,

And both that morning equally lay
In leaves no step had trodden black.
Oh, I kept the first for another day!
Yet knowing how way leads on to way,
I doubted if I should ever come back.

I shall be telling this with a sigh
Somewhere ages and ages hence:
Two roads diverged in a wood, and I—
I took the one less traveled by,
And that has made all the difference.

Acquainted with the Night

I have been one acquainted with the night.
I have walked out in rain—and back in rain.
I have outwalked the furthest city light.

I have looked down the saddest city lane.
I have passed by the watchman on his beat
And dropped my eyes, unwilling to explain.

I have stood still and stopped the sound of feet
When far away an interrupted cry
Came over houses from another street,

But not to call me back or say good-by;
And further still at an unearthly height
One luminary clock against the sky

Proclaimed the time was neither wrong nor right.
I have been one acquainted with the night.

Hughes Mearns (1875–1965)

Antigonish

As I was going up the stair
    I met a man who wasn't there!
He wasn't there again to-day!
    I wish, I *wish* he'd stay away!

Adelaide Crapsey (1878–1914)

November Night

Listen . . .
With faint dry sound,
Like steps of passing ghosts,
The leaves, frost-crisp'd, break from the trees
And fall.

The Warning

Just now,
Out of the strange
Still dusk . . . as strange, as still . . .
A white moth flew . . . Why am I grown
So cold?

John Masefield (1878–1967)

Sea Fever

I must go down to the seas again, to the lonely sea and the sky,
And all I ask is a tall ship and a star to steer her by;
And the wheel's kick and the wind's song and the white sail's shaking,
And a grey mist on the sea's face, and a grey dawn breaking.

I must go down to the seas again, for the call of the running tide
Is a wild call and a clear call that may not be denied;
And all I ask is a windy day with the white clouds flying,
And the flung spray and the blown spume, and the sea-gulls crying.

I must go down to the seas again, to the vagrant gypsy life,
To the gull's way and the whale's way where the wind's like a whetted
    knife;
And all I ask is a merry yarn from a laughing fellow-rover,
And quiet sleep and a sweet dream when the long trick's over.

Carl Sandburg (1878–1967)

Fog

The fog comes
on little cat feet.

It sits looking
over harbor and city
on silent haunches
and then, moves on.

Grass

Pile the bodies high at Austerlitz and Waterloo.
Shovel them under and let me work—
                I am the grass; I cover all.

And pile them high at Gettysburg
And pile them high at Ypres and Verdun.
Shovel them under and let me work.
Two years, ten years, and passengers ask the conductor:
                What place is this?
                Where are we now?

                I am the grass.
                Let me work.

Wallace Stevens (1879–1955)

The Emperor of Ice-Cream

Call the roller of big cigars,
The muscular one, and bid him whip
In kitchen cups concupiscent curds.
Let the wenches dawdle in such dress
As they are used to wear, and let the boys
Bring flowers in last month's newspapers.
Let be be finale of seem.
The only emperor is the emperor of ice-cream.

Take from the dresser of deal,
Lacking the three glass knobs, that sheet
On which she embroidered fantails once
And spread it so as to cover her face.
If her horny feet protrude, they come
To show how cold she is, and dumb.
Let the lamp affix its beam.
The only emperor is the emperor of ice-cream.

Disillusionment of Ten O'Clock

The houses are haunted
By white night-gowns.
None are green,
Or purple with green rings,
Or green with yellow rings,
Or yellow with blue rings.

None of them are strange,
With socks of lace
And beaded ceintures.
People are not going
To dream of baboons and periwinkles.
Only, here and there, an old sailor,
Drunk and asleep in his boots,
Catches tigers
In red weather.

William Carlos Williams (1883–1963)

The Red Wheelbarrow

so much depends
upon

a red wheel
barrow

glazed with rain
water

beside the white
chickens

Sara Teasdale (1884–1933)

The Kiss

I hoped that he would love me,
    And he has kissed my mouth,
But I am like a stricken bird
    That cannot reach the south.

For though I know he loves me,
    To-night my heart is sad;
His kiss was not so wonderful
    As all the dreams I had.

I Shall Not Care

When I am dead and over me bright April
    Shakes out her rain-drenched hair,
Though you should lean above me broken-hearted,
    I shall not care.

I shall have peace as leafy trees are peaceful,
    When rain bends down the bough,
And I shall be more silent and cold-hearted
    Than you are now.

Ezra Pound (1885–1972)

In a Station of the Metro

The apparition of these faces in the crowd;
Petals on a wet, black bough.

L'Art, 1910

Green arsenic smeared on an egg-white cloth,
Crushed strawberries! Come, let us feast our eyes.

Joyce Kilmer (1886–1918)

Trees

I think that I shall never see
A poem lovely as a tree.

A tree whose hungry mouth is prest
Against the earth's sweet flowing breast;

A tree that looks at God all day,
And lifts her leafy arms to pray;

A tree that may in Summer wear
A nest of robins in her hair;

Upon whose bosom snow has lain;
Who intimately lives with rain.

Poems are made by fools like me,
But only God can make a tree.

Rupert Brooke (1887–1915)

The Soldier

If I should die, think only this of me:
   That there's some corner of a foreign field
That is for ever England. There shall be
   In that rich earth a richer dust concealed;
A dust whom England bore, shaped, made aware,
   Gave, once, her flowers to love, her ways to roam,
A body of England's, breathing English air,
   Washed by the rivers, blest by suns of home.

And think, this heart, all evil shed away,
   A pulse in the eternal mind, no less
     Gives somewhere back the thoughts by England given;
Her sights and sounds; dreams happy as her day;
   And laughter, learnt of friends; and gentleness,
     In hearts at peace, under an English heaven.

Claude McKay (1890–1948)

Harlem Shadows

I hear the halting footsteps of a lass
   In Negro Harlem when the night lets fall
Its veil. I see the shapes of girls who pass
   Eager to heed desire's insistent call:
Ah, little dark girls, who in slippered feet
   Go prowling through the night from street to street.

Through the long night until the silver break
   Of day the little gray feet know no rest,
Through the lone night until the last snow-flake
   Has dropped from heaven upon the earth's white breast,
The dusky, half-clad girls of tired feet
   Are trudging, thinly shod, from street to street.

Ah, stern harsh world, that in the wretched way
   Of poverty, dishonor and disgrace,
Has pushed the timid little feet of clay.
   The sacred brown feet of my fallen race!
Ah, heart of me, the weary, weary feet
   In Harlem wandering from street to street.

T. S. Eliot (1888–1965)

Morning at the Window

They are rattling breakfast plates in basement kitchens,
And along the trampled edges of the street
I am aware of the damp souls of housemaids
Sprouting despondently at area gates.

The brown waves of fog toss up to me
Twisted faces from the bottom of the street,
And tear from a passer-by with muddy skirts
An aimless smile that hovers in the air
And vanishes along the level of the roofs.

The *Boston Evening Transcript*

The readers of the *Boston Evening Transcript*
Sway in the wind like a field of ripe corn.

When evening quickens faintly in the street,
Wakening the appetites of life in some
And to others bringing the *Boston Evening Transcript*,
I mount the steps and ring the bell, turning
Wearily, as one would turn to nod good-bye to Rochefoucauld,
If the street were time and he at the end of the street,
And I say, "Cousin Harriet, here is the *Boston Evening Transcript*."

Archibald MacLeish (1892–1982)

The End of the World

Quite unexpectedly as Vasserot
The armless ambidextrian was lighting
A match between his great and second toe,
And Ralph the lion was engaged in biting
The neck of Madame Sossman while the drum
Pointed, and Teeny was about to cough
In waltz-time swinging Jocko by the thumb—
Quite unexpectedly the top blew off:

And there, there overhead, there, there hung over
Those thousands of white faces, those dazed eyes,
There in the starless dark the poise, the hover,
There with vast wings across the canceled skies,

There in the sudden blackness the black pall
Of nothing, nothing, nothing—nothing at all.

Edna St. Vincent Millay (1892–1950)

First Fig

My candle burns at both ends;
   It will not last the night;
But ah, my foes and oh, my friends—
   It gives a lovely light.

Euclid Alone Has Looked on Beauty Bare

Euclid alone has looked on Beauty bare.
Let all who prate of Beauty hold their peace,
And lay them prone upon the earth and cease
To ponder on themselves, the while they stare
At nothing, intricately drawn nowhere
In shapes of shifting lineage; let geese
Gabble and hiss, but heroes seek release
From dusty bondage into luminous air.
O blinding hour, O holy, terrible day,
When first the shaft into his vision shone
Of light anatomized! Euclid alone
Has looked on Beauty bare. Fortunate they
Who, though once only and then but far away,
Have heard her massive sandal set on stone.

Wilfred Owen (1893–1982)

Anthem for Doomed Youth

What passing-bells for these who die as cattle?
   Only the monstrous anger of the guns.
   Only the stuttering rifles' rapid rattle
Can patter out their hasty orisons.
No mockeries now for them; no prayers nor bells,
   Nor any voice of mourning save the choirs,—
The shrill, demented choirs of wailing shells;
   And bugles calling for them from sad shires.

What candles may. be held to speed them all?
   Not in the hands of boys, but in their eyes
Shall shine the holy glimmers of good-byes.
   The pallor of girls' brows shall be their pall;
Their flowers the tenderness of patient minds,
And each slow dusk a drawing-down of blinds.

Langston Hughes (1902–1967)

The Negro Speaks of Rivers

I've known rivers:
I've known rivers ancient as the world and older than the flow of
   human blood in human veins.

My soul has grown deep like the rivers.

I bathed in the Euphrates when dawns were young.
I built my hut near the Congo and it lulled me to sleep.

I looked upon the Nile and raised the pyramids above it.
I heard the singing of the Mississippi when Abe Lincoln went down to
   New Orleans, and I've seen its muddy bosom turn all golden in
   the sunset.

I've known rivers:
Ancient, dusky rivers.

My soul has grown deep like the rivers.

Dylan Thomas (1914–1953)

Do Not Go Gentle into That Good Night

Do not go gentle into that good night,
Old age should burn and rave at close of day;
Rage, rage against the dying of the light.

Though wise men at their end know dark is right,
Because their words had forked no lightning they
Do not go gentle into that good night.

Good men, the last wave by, crying how bright
Their frail deeds might have danced in a green bay,
Rage, rage against the dying of the light.

Wild men who caught and sang the sun in flight,
And learn, too late, they grieved it on its way,
Do not go gentle into that good night.

Grave men, near death, who see with blinding sight
Blind eyes could blaze like meteors and be gay,
Rage, rage against the dying of the light.

And you, my father, there on the sad height,
Curse, bless, me now with your fierce tears, I pray.
Do not go gentle into that good night.
Rage, rage against the dying of the light.